WORKING WITH FAMILIES AND COMMUNITY AGENCIES TO SUPPORT STUDENTS WITH SPECIAL NEEDS

A PRACTICAL APPROACH TO SPECIAL EDUCATION FOR EVERY TEACHER

The Fundamentals of Special Education
A Practical Guide for Every Teacher

The Legal Foundations of Special Education
A Practical Guide for Every Teacher

Effective Assessment for Students With Special Needs
A Practical Guide for Every Teacher

Effective Instruction for Students With Special Needs
A Practical Guide for Every Teacher

*Working With Families and Community Agencies to
 Support Students With Special Needs*
A Practical Guide for Every Teacher

Public Policy, School Reform, and Special Education
A Practical Guide for Every Teacher

Teaching Students With Sensory Disabilities
A Practical Guide for Every Teacher

Teaching Students With Medical, Physical, and Multiple Disabilities
A Practical Guide for Every Teacher

Teaching Students With Learning Disabilities
A Practical Guide for Every Teacher

Teaching Students With Communication Disorders
A Practical Guide for Every Teacher

Teaching Students With Emotional Disturbance
A Practical Guide for Every Teacher

Teaching Students With Mental Retardation
A Practical Guide for Every Teacher

Teaching Students With Gifts and Talents
A Practical Guide for Every Teacher

Working With Families and Community Agencies to Support Students With Special Needs

A Practical Guide for Every Teacher

JIM YSSELDYKE
BOB ALGOZZINE

CORWIN PRESS
A SAGE Publications Company
Thousand Oaks, California

For information:

Corwin Press
A Sage Publications Company
2455 Teller Road
Thousand Oaks, California 91320
www.corwinpress.com

Sage Publications Ltd.
1 Oliver's Yard
55 City Road
London EC1Y 1SP
United Kingdom

Sage Publications India Pvt. Ltd.
B-42, Panchsheel Enclave
Post Box 4109
New Delhi 110 017 India

Printed in the United States of America

Library of Congress Cataloging-in-Publication Data

Ysseldyke, James E.
Working with families and community agencies to support students with special needs: A practical guide for every teacher / James E. Ysseldyke & Bob Algozzine.
    p. cm.
Includes bibliographical references and index.
ISBN 1-4129-3945-3 (cloth)
ISBN 1-4129-3898-8 (pbk.)
    1. Children with disabilities—Education. 2. Children with disabilities—Services for. 3. Special education—Parent participation. I. Algozzine, Robert. II. Title.
LC4015.Y78 2006
371.904--dc22

                                                                    2005037821

This book is printed on acid-free paper.

06   07   08   09   10   9   8   7   6   5   4   3   2   1

Acquisitions Editor:	Kylee M. Liegl
Editorial Assistant:	Nadia Kashper
Production Editor:	Denise Santoyo
Copy Editor:	Marilyn Power Scott
Typesetter:	C&M Digitals (P) Ltd.
Indexer:	Kathy Paparchontis
Cover Designer:	Michael Dubowe

Contents

About
A Practical Approach to Special Education for Every Teacher

Special education means specially designed instruction for students with unique learning needs. Students receive special education for many reasons. Students with disabilities like mental retardation, hearing impairments (including deafness), speech or language impairments, visual impairments (including blindness), emotional disturbance, orthopedic impairments, autism, traumatic brain injury, other health impairments, or specific learning disabilities are entitled to special education services. Students who are gifted and talented also receive special education. Special education services are delivered in many settings, including regular classes, resource rooms, and separate classes. The 13 books of this collection will help you teach students with disabilities and those with gifts and talents. Each book focuses on a specific area of special education and can be used individually or in conjunction with all or some of the other books. Six of the books provide the background and content knowledge you need in order to work effectively with all students with unique learning needs:

Book 1: The Fundamentals of Special Education

Book 2: The Legal Foundations of Special Education

Book 3: Effective Assessment for Students With Special Needs

Book 4: Effective Instruction for Students With Special Needs

Book 5: Working With Families and Community Agencies to Support Students With Special Needs

Book 6: Public Policy, School Reform, and Special Education

Seven of the books focus on teaching specific groups of students who receive special education:

Book 7:   Teaching Students With Sensory Disabilities

Book 8:   Teaching Students With Medical, Physical, and Multiple Disabilities

Book 9:   Teaching Students With Learning Disabilities

Book 10: Teaching Students With Communication Disorders

Book 11: Teaching Students With Emotional Disturbance

Book 12: Teaching Students With Mental Retardation

Book 13: Teaching Students With Gifts and Talents

All of the books in *A Practical Approach to Special Education for Every Teacher* will help you to make a difference in the lives of all students, especially those with unique learning needs.

ACKNOWLEDGMENTS

The approach we take in *A Practical Approach to Special Education for Every Teacher* is an effort to change how professionals learn about special education. The 13 separate books are a result of prodding from our students and from professionals in the field to provide a set of materials that "cut to the chase" in teaching them about students with disabilities and about building the capacity of systems to meet those students' needs. Teachers told us that in their classes they always confront students with special learning needs, and students their school district has assigned a label to (e.g. students with learning disabilities). Our students and the professionals we worked with wanted a very practical set of texts that gave them the necessary **information** *about* **the students** (e.g., federal definitions, student characteristics) and specific **information on** *what to do about* **the students** (assessment and teaching strategies, approaches that work). They also wanted the opportunity to purchase "parts" of textbooks rather than entire texts, to learn what they needed.

The production of this collection would not have been possible without the support and assistance of many colleagues. Professionals associated with Corwin Press—Faye Zucker, Kylee Liegl, Robb Clouse—helped us work through the idea of introducing special education differently, and their support in helping us do it is deeply appreciated.

Faye Ysseldyke and Kate Algozzine, our children, and our grandchildren also deserve recognition. They have made the problems associated with writing books and other labors like this very easy to diminish, deal with, or dismiss. Every day in every way they enrich our lives and make us better. We are grateful for them.

About the Authors

Jim Ysseldyke, PhD, is Birkmaier Professor in the Department of Educational Psychology, Director of the School Psychology Program and Director of the Center for Reading Research at the University of Minnesota. Widely requested as a staff developer and conference speaker, Ysseldyke brings more than 30 years of research and teaching experience to educational professionals around the globe.

As the former director of the federally funded National Center on Educational Outcomes, Ysseldyke conducted research and provided technical support that helped to boost the academic performance of students with disabilities and improve school assessment techniques nationally. Today, he continues to work to improve the education of students with disabilities.

The author of more than 300 publications on special education and school psychology, Ysseldyke is best known for his textbooks on assessment, effective instruction, issues in special education, and other cutting-edge areas of education and school psychology. With *A Practical Approach to Special Education for Every Teacher*, Ysseldyke seeks to equip educators with practical knowledge and methods that will help them to better engage students in exploring—and meeting—all their potentials.

Bob Algozzine, PhD, is Professor in the Department of Educational Leadership and project codirector of the U.S. Department of Education–supported Behavior & Reading Improvement Center. With 25 years of research experience and extensive firsthand knowledge of teaching students classified as seriously emotionally disturbed (and other equally useless terms), Algozzine is a uniquely qualified staff developer, conference speaker, and teacher of behavior management and effective teaching courses.

As an active partner and collaborator with professionals in the Charlotte-Mecklenburg schools in North Carolina and as an editor of several journals focused on special education, Algozzine keeps his finger on the pulse of current special education practice. He has written more than 250 manuscripts on special education topics, authoring many popular books and textbooks on how to manage emotional and social behavior problems. Through *A Practical Approach to Special Education for Every Teacher*, Algozzine hopes to continue to help improve the lives of students with special needs—and the professionals who teach them.

Self-Assessment 1

Before you begin this book, check your knowledge of the content being covered. Choose the best answer for each of the following questions.

1. As a result of the Public Law 98–199 passed in 1984, a child with special needs can receive comprehensive services

   a. From birth

   b. From the age of 1 year

   c. From the age of 2 years

   d. From the age of 3 years

2. What is the name of the federally funded early intervention program specially tailored for children from economically disadvantaged families?

   a. Success for All

   b. Head Start

   c. Hope for Every Child

   d. No Child Left Behind

3. The law requires that every child below the age of 5 years who has a disability have an

   a. Individualized life-stage plan

   b. Individualized transition plan

   c. Individualized education program

   d. Individualized family service plan

4. _____ services refer to services provided to the child in settings for early intervention programs.

   a. Direct

   b. Indirect

   c. Center-based

   d. Home-based

5. Which one of the following is NOT a student characteristic associated with a greater likelihood of students dropping out of school?

   a. Gender

   b. Learning style

   c. Size of the school

   d. Socioeconomic status

6. Which type of employment do professionals consider to be the goal of all young adults with disabilities?

   a. Full-time employment

   b. Sheltered employment

   c. Supported employment

   d. Competitive employment

7. Which one of the following is the term stated in the Education for All Handicapped Children Act that requires that children be placed in an educational setting as much like the regular classroom as possible?

   a. Deinstitutionalization

   b. Inclusion

   c. Least restrictive environment

   d. Mainstreaming

8. Which one of the following is viewed by professionals in special education as violating the ideal of "life as much like normal as possible" principle of the Individuals with Disabilities Act?

    a. Foster homes

    b. Group homes

    c. Residential institutions

    d. Alternative living units

9. _____ are programs which provide high school students exposure to actual working situations and the opportunity to gain work experience.

    a. Community transition program

    b. School-based enterprises

    c. Tech-prep programs

    d. Youth apprenticeships

10. The prevailing belief about students with disabilities is that

    a. Advanced schooling is too pressuring for them.

    b. They should strive to be as independent as possible.

    c. They should be placed in residential institutions as early as possible.

    d. They should work in self-contained environment specially tailored to their needs.

REFLECTION

After you answer the multiple-choice questions, think about how you would answer the following questions:

- What is early intervention? Why is it important to provide early intervention programs to children with special needs?
- What are the advantages and disadvantages of

  a. Home-based programs

  b. Center-based programs?
- What are the different forms of family involvement?
- How successful have you been encouraging family involvement in your school? What are some barriers to home-school collaboration? What can be done to overcome these barriers?

Introduction to
Working With Families and Community Agencies to Support Students With Special Needs

> **Fred**, a 1991 high school graduate, was born with developmental disabilities. There were no early childhood special education (ECSE) services in the early 1970s, but Fred's mother found a teacher who was willing to provide him with preschool enrichment two hours a day, three days a week. Fred attended self-contained special education classes during his school years but attended general education art and physical education classes. He also attended some vocational classes.
>
> Transition planning for Fred began two years before he was to leave high school. At that time, he had a county developmental disability social worker and a counselor from the state department of vocational rehabilitation services. Fred spent part of each school day at the county technical college, working on vocational skills in the technical center. Fred received training in the food industry career program where he learned about food preparation, busing, dishwashing, and cleaning. This career program helped provide Fred with the background necessary to find a job in his community.

As Fred's story illustrates, disabilities do not start and end when students enter and leave school. Besides, students with disabilities spend only about 20 percent of a 24-hour day in school. If these statements were not true, we may not need to write this book. We'd assume that what students learn is a function of what we do for them in school. Instead, in this book, we address two of the most exciting parts of working with students with disabilities:

Life stage issues (early intervention and transition)

Collaboration (working with families and professionals)

In short, we talk about aspects of the larger context of students' lives outside school and how these aspects interact with and influence instruction. If you are going to be a teacher, you will have to consider early intervention, transition, working with families, and working with the broader educational community.

EARLY INTERVENTION

Educators and developmental psychologists recognize the importance of early development and early experience to later life success. In the first part of this book, we describe interventions early in children's lives intended to prevent later school difficulties. We address the importance of such early intervention, especially in light of the major demographic changes taking place in society.

PLANNING FOR TRANSITION

In an age in which Americans plan everything, it is not surprising that major consideration is being given to the transition children undergo from home to school and the transition of adolescents with disabilities from school to work. Much consideration is given to the skills that will enable students with disabilities to get jobs, to function in society, and generally to improve the quality of their lives. In the second part of this book we address the many transitions that students with disabilities must make during their lives.

Family Involvement

Family involvement is not only a legal imperative, but it also makes sense. Over the past 20 years or so, educators have talked a great deal about empowering families and involving them in their children's educational programs. Recently, major efforts have been undertaken to make this happen. We devote a section of this book to involving families and considerations in working with them.

Community Collaboration

Schools and school personnel cannot meet all of the challenges now confronting them without close working relationships with business and community leaders and personnel from community agencies and services. This book describes current efforts to work in a collaborative manner to meet the concerns and challenges of the day.

1

What Should Every Teacher Know About Early Childhood Intervention?

M s. Dennis, a kindergarten teacher, was finding that many of the students entering her class already had mastered the content she was prepared to present. By checking with some of the parents, she discovered that the local preschool programs had adopted a firm stance on academics in response to parents' requests that they better prepare children for kindergarten. The kindergarten teacher was considering restructuring the academic year in response to this new population of students with well-developed skills.

MORE CHILDREN ATTEND PRESCHOOL

From 1987 to 2000 (National Center for Education Statistics, 2002), preprimary enrollment increased in the United States by about 33 percent for children between the ages of 3 and 5. By 2000, more than half of the children between ages 3 and 5 were enrolled in nursery school or kindergarten classes. Of this total, about

43 percent of 3-year-olds, 64 percent of 4-year-olds, and 92 percent of 5-year-olds were enrolled in preprimary educational programs. In 2000–2001, 35 percent of public elementary schools offered kindergarten and over 800,000 children participated (National Center for Education Statistics, 2002). During 2000–2001 about 65 percent of all children younger than 6 years of age who were not enrolled in kindergarten regularly participated in early educational programs or some type of child care (National Institute for Early Education Research, 2002). By and large, these students are better prepared for school and are more advanced academically than students who started school five to ten years ago.

MORE CHILDREN NEED PROGRAMS

At the same time that there are more preschool programs, there are more students in need of the programs. Fetal alcohol syndrome and alcohol-related birth defects are on the rise. Babies born with AIDS are increasing in number each year, and so are babies with medical problems resulting from their mothers' addiction to cocaine. Infants who are medically fragile are surviving through extraordinary medical interventions but then may face life with significant mental and physical impairments. Even children born healthy may face poverty, homelessness, or physical abuse. It is argued that we ought to intervene early in the lives of children to prevent later problems and to enable them to enter school ready to learn. The first National Educational Goal was that by the year 2000, all children would start school ready to learn. This goal has still not been met.

MORE PRESCHOOLERS RECEIVE SPECIAL EDUCATION SERVICES

The increase in the numbers of children ages 3–5 who received special education services under the Individuals With Disabilities Education Act (IDEA; 1997) during the 1992–1993, 1996–1997, and 2000–2001 (most recent available) school years is shown in

Figure 1.1   Number of Preschoolers Receiving Services
Under IDEA During the 1992–1993, 1996–1997,
and 2000–2001 School Years

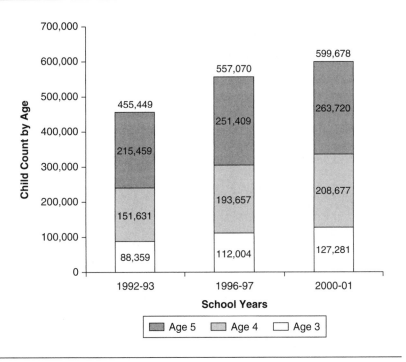

Source: U.S. Department of Education (2002).

Figure 1.1. Illustrated is the fact that over time, more and more preschoolers are receiving special education services.

FEDERAL LAWS AND INCENTIVES

In 1968 the Handicapped Children's Early Education Assistance Act (Public Law 90–538) was passed. It was the first law that provided federal funds for innovative programs for preschool children with disabilities. By 1973 Head Start and other federally funded programs were required to keep at least 10 percent of their spaces available for children with disabilities. The Education for All Handicapped Children Act of 1975 (Public

Law 94–142) mandated services for all 3- to 5-year-olds by 1980; state law already provided services for children without disabilities in that age group. It also provided incentive grants to states for improving early childhood special education programs.

In 1984, Public Law 98–199 (Education of the Handicapped 1983) made funds available to states to develop comprehensive services for children with special needs from birth to age 5. Two years later, President Reagan signed into law the amendments to the Education for All Handicapped Children Act (Public Law 99–457). This legislation expanded services to children with disabilities who are under age 5. It mandated that schools must have on file for each preschool child with a disability an **individualized family service plan (IFSP)**. An IFSP is a kind of IEP (individualized education program) for young children.

The amendments to the Education for All Handicapped Children Act also authorized the distribution of federal funds to help states provide special education to very young children and guaranteed a free, appropriate education to all preschoolers with disabilities. This law also made special education for young children with disabilities compulsory, and parents became an important part of the educational program. The provisions of this law were incorporated into the amendments of the Individuals With Disabilities Education Act (1997).

DIRECT AND INDIRECT SERVICES

Settings for early intervention programs differ, and the nature of services provided in the settings is diverse. When the services are provided to the child, they are called **direct services;** when they are provided to another person, such as a parent, who in turn serves the child, they are called **indirect services**.

HOME-BASED PROGRAMS

Some early childhood special education (ECSE) programs are **home based**, especially for very young children (birth to age 3).

When this is the case, school personnel visit the home regularly, either to provide direct services or to educate families who in turn educate the young children. In some home-based programs, the visits occur weekly and are designed primarily to improve the families' skills in working with their children. The type of service depends on the type of disability and the willingness of the family to teach the child. Families also receive indirect services in some home-based programs. Specially trained teachers make recommendations for training, organize groups of parents with similar concerns, and help families monitor the progress of the intervention they are providing.

Hospital-Based or Center-Based Programs

In other instances the programs are **hospital based** or **center based**. In hospital settings, the services may be provided directly to the child or to hospital personnel who work with the child. In center-based programs, the family brings the child to a center for direct or indirect services. The center may be at a hospital, school, day care center, clinic or other facility. Once there, families may work with their children under the guidance of specially trained professionals, or they may observe others working with their children. In some center-based programs, groups of parents meet to share concerns and provide support for one another. Other centers are organized primarily as referral sources for services available locally.

For students who do not need to be hospitalized, the choice is between home-based and center-based intervention programs, both of which have advantages and disadvantages. At home, the child learns in a natural environment surrounded by family members who often can spend more time working with the child at home than they can at a center. Problems associated with transportation, care of other children, and general family disruption are minimized when special education is carried out at home. Home-based programs, however, have several disadvantages, including the following:

Success depends heavily on the family's cooperation.

Children from homes where both parents work or homes where there is one parent and that parent works may be less likely to receive special education at home.

Being at home limits opportunities for interaction with other adults and children.

A center-based approach provides varied types of help at a central location. Professionals from several disciplines, such as medicine, psychology, occupational therapy, speech and language pathology, and education, work together to assess and teach the child. The program benefits from periodic meetings to discuss progress and plan future interventions. The disadvantages of center-based intervention include the time and expense of transportation, the cost of maintaining a center, and the likelihood of less family involvement.

Regardless of which approach is taken (and many professionals combine them), the curriculum generally is the same. We teach young children with disabilities to improve their language, motor, self-help, communication, preacademic, and cognitive skills. We also try to improve their self-concepts, creativity, motivation to succeed, and general readiness for social interaction in school.

A generation ago, families of preschool children with disabilities were offered little help. Today, public special education is available from birth to age 21, and early childhood programs are a rapidly growing part of special education.

DOES EARLY INTERVENTION HELP?

Policy reports have regularly noted the cost-effectiveness and cost benefits derived from early intervention. For example, the Committee for Economic Development (1991) stated

> Quality preschool programs clearly provide one of the most cost-effective strategies for lowering the drop out rate and helping at-risk children to become more effective learners and productive citizens. It has been shown that for every $1 spent on a comprehensive and intensive

preschool program for the disadvantaged, society saves up to $6 in the long-term costs of welfare, remedial education, teen pregnancy, and crime. (p. 28)

Head Start

Head Start is the most widely publicized and publicly recognized early intervention for children. It is designed to be used with those who are economically disadvantaged. In a study of the extent to which Head Start helped children, Lee, Schnur, and Brooks-Gunn (1988) demonstrated that children who participated in Head Start showed significant short-term gains but were still behind their peers in absolute cognitive levels after a year in the program. Currie and Thomas (1996) showed that Head Start is associated with large and significant gains in test scores among both whites and African Americans. Yet gains are quickly lost among African Americans.

Haskins (1989) wrote a cautionary paper arguing that research had shown that model preschool programs and Head Start have an immediate impact on the cognitive test scores and social development of students but that the gains diminish over the first few years of public schooling. He argues that "There is limited put provocative evidence that model programs may have positive effects on life success measures such as teen pregnancy, delinquency, welfare use, and employment, but there is virtually no evidence linking Head Start attendance with any of these variables" (p. 274). It may be very difficult to demonstrate direct links between preschool intervention and later life success, because it would be necessary to follow students for 20 or more years to answer the necessary cost-benefit questions. Most people would rather err in the direction of providing unnecessary yet nonharmful services than wait 20 years for evidence that the services had a beneficial effect.

Ypsilanti Perry Preschool Project

One of the most extensive evaluations of early childhood services was performed by analyzing the effects of the Ypsilanti

Perry Preschool Project, a service for economically disadvantaged 3- and 4-year-old children in Ypsilanti, Michigan. It was shown that a substantial proportion of the costs for providing preschool services were recovered because children did not need such extensive special education support once they entered school. In addition, none of the graduates of the Perry Preschool Project required institutional placement. Perry Preschool graduates were also shown to have higher projected lifetime earnings than similar children who did not receive the services. The evaluation showed that early intervention resulted in a savings per child of $14,819. Berrueta-Clement, Schweinhart, Barnett, Epstein, and Weikart (1984) reported that this amounted to a 243 percent return on original dollar investment.

2

What Are Transition Services and When Are They Necessary?

L ife is a series of transitions. People make the transitions from one class to another while in school and most survive the transition between childhood and adulthood known as adolescence. People also move from one location to another, from one type of relationship to another, or from student life to work life. These transitions, although often stressful, are made without much difficulty by most persons. In the 1980s, however, professionals joined parents in realizing that not all individuals make transitions easily. This realization led to an emphasis on the transition process and the difficulties many individuals with disabilities had in successfully accomplishing transitions. Special efforts were deemed necessary to successfully transition the individual with special needs.

TYPES OF TRANSITIONS

The transition from school to adulthood has received considerable attention from special educators. Schools are required by law to have **transition plans** for students with disabilities. These transition plans are for movement from school to work or other postschool environments. Individuals with disabilities make other critical transitions as well. For example, they must accomplish the transition from home to school in the first place and then negotiate numerous transitions within school. There are transitions from one grade level or type of school to another and unique transitions, such as those from one type of school placement to another, one school to another, general to special education settings, and special to general education settings.

Transition Into School

The first school-related transition is that from preschool into a formal K–12 education system. An important consideration at this time of transition is whether students with disabilities should be categorized.

It is not necessary to label students "disabled" to allow them to attend a preschool program for students with disabilities. Yet often, attendance in the program is a form of labeling. One of the authors of this book has had the experience of sitting in a teachers' lounge listening to a kindergarten teacher lament the fact that she was getting four children from the local preschool program for students with disabilities. Even before seeing or visiting with the children, she anticipated difficulty. Professional research literature tells us that when students are expected to experience difficulty, they often do so.

Thurlow et al. (1986) conducted a detailed case study analysis of what happened to young children as they left preschool and entered kindergarten. The researchers found extreme variability in the transition process. In some districts, program staff visited with staff of a child's elementary program, discussing in detail the child's strengths and weaknesses and recommending techniques for teaching the child successfully. In one district, all information related to the child's participation in the early childhood special education program was deleted from the records, and the child was sent to the elementary school without indication of previous special education services. Seldom did those who served students with disabilities follow up on the performances of the children in elementary school.

Current information on how to ensure a smooth transition from preschool to elementary school is not consistent. In particular, no evidence exists of the effects, whether positive or adverse, of informing kindergarten teachers that students have been identified as disabled. We do not know whether this awareness biases the teachers' expectations for the children's performance or whether it helps the children.

Transitions During School

Many transitions occur as students get older—from smaller to larger classes, from smaller to larger buildings, and from having a single teacher all day to having seven or eight teachers each day. Perhaps because these transitions seem to be made with relative ease, there has been limited research on them. Yet transitions probably are made more easily by students who are not disabled than by those with disabilities. Teachers need to work together to facilitate smooth transitions by students with disabilities.

Everyday Transitions

Students with disabilities often move among school settings for their particular educational experiences. They may have to go to other rooms or buildings rather than spending an entire day with a single teacher. Students with disabilities usually are taught by more than one teacher, or they meet with a number of specialists: with an occupational therapist in the morning and a special education teacher in the afternoon, or with two special education teachers—one who specializes in academics and one who specializes in behavior. Students who leave general education classrooms have to adjust to dealing with more than one teacher and also to entering and leaving curriculum activities when other students do not. In addition, they must explain to other students why they leave the classroom and for what purpose.

Transition in General Education Classrooms

Students who do not leave the general education classroom but find themselves with the special education teacher inside it may not have to make as many transition adjustments as other students with disabilities, but the adjustments may still be considerable. When this type of integrated service is used by the special education teacher as another way to deliver typical special education (e.g., using alternative materials, drilling basic facts), students must learn to concentrate when others in the class are engaged in completely different tasks.

It is important that teachers consider how students are going to make up the work they miss when they leave a classroom to receive special services. Much consideration must also be given to how students will move among services.

Dropping Out of School

We include a separate section on dropping out because so many students with disabilities do it. Dropping out is a significant transition, perhaps the most negative of possible school outcomes. Schooling is compulsory by law; schools are expected to serve all students.

How many students end their school careers by dropping out? There is no agreement on rate and no agreement on a definition of dropping out. Dropping out is associated with negative personal outcomes, such as unemployment, low income and lifetime earnings, limited cognitive growth, and limited scholastic achievement.

In 2002, 13 percent of all persons aged 16–24 were neither enrolled in school nor working. This is a decrease from 16 percent in 1986. Dropout percentages are higher for students with disabilities. In 1999–2000, 29.4 percent of students with disabilities dropped out of school (U.S. Department of Education, 2002). At the same time, though, increasing numbers of students with disabilities are completing school with a standard diploma. The numbers of students in the various disability categories who graduated with a standard diploma and the percentage who dropped out of school is shown in Table 2.1.

Table 2.1 Number and Percentage of Students Aged 14 and Older With Disabilities Graduating With a Standard Diploma or Dropping Out, 1999–2000, in the State of Washington

Disability Category	Graduated With a Standard Diploma		Dropped Out	
	Number	Percentage	Number	Percentage
Specific learning disabilities	109,012	62.1	48,490	27.6
Speech or language impairments	4,802	66.1	1,787	24.6
Mental retardation	16,425	39.5	10,812	26.0
Emotional disturbance	14,842	40.1	19,032	51.4
Multiple disabilities	2,676	48.0	896	16.1
Hearing impairments	2,862	68.4	620	14.8
Orthopedic impairments	2,055	62.5	506	15.4
Other health impairments	7,325	67.7	2,423	22.4
Visual impairments	1,157	73.4	187	11.9
Autism	578	47.3	135	11.1
Deaf-blindness	47	48.5	10	10.3
Traumatic brain injury	799	65.3	221	18.1
All disabilities	162,580	56.2	85,119	29.4

Notes: The percentages in this table were calculated by dividing the number of students aged 14 and older who graduated with a standard diploma by the number of students aged 14 and older who are known to have left special education (i.e., graduated with a standard diploma, received a certificate of completion, reached the maximum age for services, died, or dropped out).

Source: U.S. Department of Education (2002).

Personnel at Stanford Research Institute International (Wagner, 1991) supported earlier findings that students with disabilities leave school more often than those without disabilities. Notably quick to leave are students with mild to moderate disabilities, especially those who have been declared emotionally disturbed. Note in Table 2.1 the large percentage of students with emotional disturbance who drop out (51.4). Major findings of the National Longitudinal Transition Study (Wagner, 1991) were the following:

A sizable percentage of students with disabilities drop out of school—a significantly higher percentage than among typical students. The drop out problem is particularly acute for students with certain disabilities—those classified as having serious emotional disturbance, learning disabilities, speech impairments, or mental retardation.

Dropping out of school is the culmination of a cluster of school performance problems, including high absenteeism and poor grade performance.

A variety of student characteristics and behaviors are associated with poor school performance and a higher likelihood that students will drop out. For example, males were significantly more likely than females to have failed courses, and lowered socioeconomic status was associated with several aspects of poor performance. Students who belonged to school or community groups had significantly better school performance and a lower probability of dropping out. Youth with disciplinary problems had poorer school performance on all measures. Understanding these risk factors can help schools target drop-out prevention programs to students most prone to early school leaving.

Dropping out is not a function solely of student and family factors. There are significant relationships between aspects of students' school programs and student outcomes. For example, students who attended larger schools and those who spent relatively more time in general education classes were more likely to fail courses. Students with disabilities who took occupationally oriented vocational training had significantly lower absenteeism and were significantly less likely than others to have dropped out of school. Schools can make a difference in their students' performance. Schools can increase the likelihood that students will finish school. (U.S. Department of Education, 1992, pp. xxi, 81)

Much can be done to avert dropout. In general, improved interventions early in school life are required. Educators have been working since the mid-1960s to try to reduce the numbers of students who drop out of school, especially those with disabilities. But they have not had much success.

Post-School Transition

A compelling need exists to improve the outcomes for students with disabilities. In an effort to do so, Congress added the requirement in 1990 of specifying in a student's individualized education program (IEP) the services that would be provided to aid the transition from school to adult life. This part of the IEP, known as the **individualized transition plan (ITP)**, helps to focus educators' attention on outcomes and the preparedness of students to assume productive adult lives. Section 602 of the Individuals With Disabilities Education Act defines **transition services** as

a coordinated set of activities for a student, designed within an outcome-oriented process, which promotes movement from school to post-school activities, including post-secondary education, vocational training, integrated employment (including supported employment), continuing and adult education services, independent living, or community participation. The coordinated set of activities shall be based upon the individual student's needs, taking into account the student's preferences and interests, and shall include instruction, community experiences, the development of employment and other post-school adult living objectives, and when appropriate, acquisition of daily living skills and functional vocational evaluation (Individuals With Disabilities Education Act, 1997).

EMPLOYMENT AND FINANCIAL INDEPENDENCE

When students with disabilities leave school, most are unemployed or underemployed. Only one-third of people with disabilities between the ages of 16–64 are working, and of those working, three-fourths have part-time jobs (Wagner, D'Amico, Marder, Newman, & Blackorby, 1992). Employment is the single most important concern of those who work with older people who are disabled. School personnel report that adults with disabilities need vocational training, placement, and evaluation services more than they need transition or postemployment services.

The National Longitudinal Transition Study (Wagner, Blackorby, Cameto, Hebbler, & Newman, 1993) gathered data on the extent to which people who left school were moving toward independence within the five years following school. The data illustrate that in the three to five years after leaving school, about half of students with disabilities move toward greater independence. About 32 percent remain stable, while about 18 percent move toward less independence. Categories in which the fewest students moved toward independence are deaf-blindness and multiple disabilities. Differences in movement toward independence are evident for students who graduated, aged out, and dropped out of school, with graduates consistently more likely to move toward independence than those aging out or dropping out.

Competitive Employment

The most common work experience for people with disabilities is in sheltered and supported employment settings, not competitive employment. **Competitive employment** means that the individual's work is valued by the employer and is performed in an integrated setting with coworkers who are not disabled, and the individual earns at or above the federal minimum wage (Rusch, Chadsey-Rusch, & Lagomarcino, 1987). Despite the low percentage of adults who are disabled in competitive employment settings, most professionals agree that competitive employment should be the goal of all young adults with disabilities.

Sheltered and Supported Employment

Sheltered employment is work in a self-contained environment in which people who are exceptional are trained and paid for their output. Some sheltered workshops provide training for work that is performed outside the special setting. Others are permanent work settings for the exceptional people who work there.

Supported employment is a relatively new concept that is designed for individuals with disabilities who need help finding, performing, and holding a job. Professionals who provide supported employment assistance do one or more of the following tasks:

Assist during job placement efforts (plan transportation, identify appropriate jobs, match skills to available jobs, communicate with social service agencies)

Provide on-the-job training and assistance (train in work skills, provide social skills and job site training, work with coworkers); the person who does this is usually called **a job coach**.

Monitor job performance (obtain regular feedback from employers, identify levels of performance and need for further training)

Provide evaluation and follow-up experiences (determine employer's satisfaction, communicate with employee periodically, help with future job placements)

Professionals in supported employment activities spend most of their time at the job sites where people with disabilities work. Supported employment specialists also spend time working with families and exceptional people in training centers or at their homes.

People with disabilities are much more likely to find and keep jobs today than they were even a few years ago, largely because families and professionals have worked to give them opportunities to become contributing members of society.

CONTINUED EDUCATION

As people with disabilities grow older, their opportunities for education are restricted. The characteristics that lead them to special services during childhood often become barriers to education in adulthood. Adults with disabilities view their education and training needs as less important than their employment and personal or social service needs. They often don't realize that they may need further education services after school. People with visual disabilities, medical or physical impairments, and multiple disabilities may have twice as many needs as people with learning disabilities, communication disorders, or serious emotional disturbance. In addition, individuals with sensory disabilities may need professional readers or interpreters.

More and more students with disabilities are entering colleges, community colleges, vocational schools, and advanced technical schools with accessible and intensive programs for exceptional students. Many factors have contributed to the emergence of these specialized educational programs (Mangrum & Strichart, 1984):

- Many students with disabilities graduate from high school and are eligible to enter college; the support they received in elementary school and high school has been extended in many college programs.
- The realization that college is a viable goal for students with disabilities has led many parents and professionals to advocate for special programs in colleges and universities.
- The interest of exceptional students in advanced schooling has brought pressure on institutions of higher learning to develop programs to meet these students' unique educational needs.
- There are not enough programs. Although more programs are available to students with learning disabilities than to those in other categories, the need for a greater number of continuing education alternatives is still apparent. Recognition of the situation is stimulating additional programs.

- The movement toward open admission policies has led many students to seek enrollment who at an earlier time might have feared rejection.
- With higher education enrollments dropping, students with disabilities are potential new consumers of postsecondary education; this financial incentive has stimulated program development for exceptional college students.

3

What Living Arrangements Are Available to Adults With Special Needs?

Exceptional people are moving out into the world. The transition from school to work includes dealing with independent-living responsibilities and residential needs. People with disabilities often worry about where and with whom they will live. They wonder whether they will always have to live with their families, whether they will ever have a room of their own, and whether they will be able to live in an apartment or home. Not long ago, people who were moderately and severely disabled lived primarily in large state hospitals and institutions. For over 200 years, institutional placement of people who were retarded, deaf, blind, or disabled in other ways was the primary means of intervention. Today, large numbers of people with disabilities still live in institutional settings, but other options are available for those who do not wish to live at home with their families.

GROUP HOMES

The practice of **mainstreaming** or **inclusion** (educating students with exceptionalities in the general education classroom whenever possible) began when teachers and other professionals implemented the least restrictive environment principle of the Education for All Handicapped Children Act (Public Law 94–142). In school settings, **least restrictive environment (LRE)** means that students who are exceptional receive all or part of their educational experiences in classrooms that are as much like normal as possible. **Deinstitutionalization** is the implementation of the LRE principle in residential facilities. It moves people with disabilities out of institutions into smaller community-based settings that are as much like normal living arrangements as possible.

Group homes are a community-based residential alternative that provides family-style living for many people who are disabled. They usually are located in residential neighborhoods, near shopping and public transportation. The number of people living in each home varies from 3 or 4 to as many as 15 or 20. Generally, specially trained professionals serve as house parents. Some group homes are primarily long-term residential placements. People in them are expected to develop independent living skills and often work outside the home in sheltered workshops or businesses in the community. Other group homes are intermediate-care facilities, where residents are supposed to learn the skills they need to move to more independent living arrangements, such as foster homes and supervised apartments.

Group homes offer a positive environment, but they sometimes create controversy in their surrounding communities. Here's how one town in North Carolina reacted to plans for a small group home:

> Some residents of Echo Farms, a golf subdivision in Wilmington off Carolina Beach Road, are trying to stop a home for the mentally retarded from locating in their neighborhood.
>
> At issue is the intended use of a brick house at 220 Dorchester Place. The owner, Charles Woodard of Goldsboro, plans to build an intermediate care facility for the mentally retarded.
>
> About 50 residents met Tuesday night for about two hours at the Echo Farms clubhouse. At the end of the meeting, representatives of the Homeowners Association said they were going to check into the situation. They also

asked a lawyer who was present to check on whether Woodard had followed proper procedure before starting to work on the facility. . . . Mitwol [the lawyer] said he would make certain that Woodard had followed all procedures correctly.

"I think it would behoove all of you folks to hold his feet to the fire on this," he said. "If they didn't follow the rules, they're out." (*Wilmington Morning Star* 1988, p. 1C)

Controlling and countering this type of stereotyped thinking and discrimination remains a challenge for all of us.

ALTERNATIVE LIVING UNITS

Some states have organized small group homes of two or three residents as an alternative to more costly homes for larger groups of people with disabilities. An **alternative living unit (ALU)** is ideal for providing a more personal environment for training and an easier structure for supervision. The amount of service provided in these settings varies with the residents' needs. People with basic living skills may need a counselor to help with specific activities and tasks, like balancing checkbooks. Others may need someone to live in to help with cooking, cleaning, and other activities.

One advantage of alternative living units is flexibility: As residents' needs change, the amount and type of support they receive can be changed; they don't have to change facilities. Professionals who support the use of alternative living units also assert that they are easier to set up than group homes and attract less attention from neighbors.

FOSTER HOMES

Some people with disabilities live with families who provide them a temporary home in return for reimbursement of their living expenses. Foster homes offer a number of positive life experiences for people with disabilities. Participating in normal family experiences, receiving personal attention, and developing close relationships with people who are not disabled are among the advantages. The primary disadvantage of foster homes is the difficulty of monitoring the quality of the experiences they provide.

INDEPENDENT LIVING

The greatest opportunity for independence and normal social interactions is provided by living in an apartment, mobile home, or other private residence. A goal of many professionals in special education is the movement of all people with disabilities to independent living facilities. They argue that group homes and foster homes are too institutional to fit their ideal of normalization.

Most adults with disabilities say that their greatest wish is to live independently. Some things that make independent living easier for them are modified controls on kitchen appliances; adjustable countertops and furniture; accessible sinks, toilets, and showers; adapted door handles; room-to-room intercoms; and easy access to emergency medical, police, and fire services. Many personal and social services are available for adults with disabilities. Those who are emotionally disturbed need more family services, for example, and transportation needs are greater for those with medical, physical, and multiple impairments.

One of the great challenges that people with disabilities face is independent mobility. Those who are not disabled often take for granted the independence that comes from being able to use automobiles, trains, airplanes, and buses. People with disabilities may have ambulation problems that make travel nearly impossible. If they are able to travel, they may be confronted by public places that are inaccessible. Adults with disabilities may be unable to obtain driving licenses, and they may have a limited circle of friends who can help them with transportation. It is critical that transition plans account for training and assistance to increase mobility.

INSTITUTIONS

For those who cannot or do not wish to live independently, in a group home, or in an alternative living unit, the option of a large-scale institution remains. Unfortunately, a residential institution that houses as many as 500 people might provide few opportunities for normal interactions. In recent years, professionals in special education have been critical of the care provided in residential facilities. They claim that residential placements violate the ideal of "life as much like normal as possible" that is at the core of the Individuals With Disabilities Education Act (IDEA). Families do not necessarily agree: Survey results of family attitudes toward residential care are generally favorable.

4

What Issues Should Be Taken Into Consideration When Working With Families?

Not many years ago, families were encouraged to place children with disabilities in institutions as early as possible. Today, they are encouraged to keep their children with special needs at home and, when they are old enough, to enroll them in neighborhood schools. Families have become active partners in the special education process in ways that were unheard of 50 years ago.

HOW EXCEPTIONALITIES AFFECT FAMILIES

In the recent past, placing a child in an institution left many families with feelings of guilt and inadequacy. Now that normalization, least restrictive environment, and inclusion are the treatments of choice, families of those with disabilities must address different concerns. The families of children who have special gifts or talents also face concerns about the social, personal, and educational needs of their children.

Effects on Family Structure

Whenever a child is born, the structure of the family changes. All families have to deal with that change, but the families of children with special needs face a special challenge. Some of their problems are unique; others differ only by degree. For example, the family of a child with special medical needs faces certain problems that families with healthy children do not face. Although all families must think about their children's future, the families of those with disabilities have special concerns.

Family Concerns

At every stage of their child's life, a family of a child who has a disability must deal with special problems. Families need accurate information about their children's conditions. They have to decide what and how to tell relatives and friends. They have to locate health and educational services. They worry about what others think about them and their children. They have to come to grips with their sadness, guilt, and anxieties. Siblings have to deal with feelings of jealousy, loss of their parents' energy and time, new responsibilities, and fears. They may worry about what their friends think and say about their siblings with disabilities.

Transition to School

Starting school is a change in routine. Most families find it difficult to adjust to that change. Exceptional children and their families find it extremely difficult. Parents of students with special needs are expected to participate in the educational program. They need to know about inclusion in general education as well as special class placement alternatives. Often they have to locate professionals who can give them help at home. In addition, they have to find afterschool care and determine the extent to which they want their children to participate in extracurricular activities. Brothers and sisters may be embarrassed, frustrated, disappointed, and even angry when a sibling who is disabled attends their own school. Siblings are often expected to participate in special training programs and support groups that compete with other social and school activities. They also have to face the limitations that the disability may have on their brother's or sister's future.

Adolescence

Adolescents with disabilities encounter increased peer rejection and personal isolation. They also often have special problems adjusting to the normal physical and emotional changes that occur during puberty. Families may have to help them cope with their feelings and arrange out-of-school activities for them.

Post-School Transition

Life after school presents a new set of challenges for individuals with special needs and their families. Finding a job and a place to live can be especially challenging, and families may worry about how their children will manage and who will care for them when they are no longer able. Brothers and sisters may face financial responsibilities for their siblings who are disabled and even be forced to assume guardianship.

CONCERNS OF FAMILIES WITH CHILDREN WHO ARE GIFTED

Families of children who are gifted share many of the same concerns as families who have children with disabilities, and many need help understanding the special needs of their gifted children. They worry that their children will be isolated, set off by their special abilities. Some families may even need to be convinced that special education is appropriate and necessary. Others seek out special programs. Although families with unusually high expectations can create problems for children and teachers, these same families can be welcome advocates in the early stages of developing programs.

Families of students who are gifted can be eager to participate in their children's education. They typically want to know how to broaden their children's experiences, how they can help their children develop a love for learning and a willingness to take intellectual risks, and how they can become actively involved in making more services available to gifted students in their communities. Others worry that they lack the skills and knowledge to meet the special needs of their children and, like all parents, worry about the effects their mistakes will have on their children's lives.

What the Research Says

Are families adversely affected by the presence of children with disabilities? Most people believe they are. Yet the research on this issue is mixed. It is risky to make blanket statements about how children with disabilities affect their families. When researchers study these families, they find that the effects differ as a function of the disability (e.g., deafness vs. blindness) and the severity of the condition. Effects also differ according to parents' views about the extent to which their children measure up to cultural standards. The interrelationships among factors that influence the effects are complex. Disabilities affect families in varying ways, and the same kind of disability may have radically different effects from one family to the next.

Change Over Time

Keep in mind that the effects children with disabilities have on their families have changed significantly with the times. In the not too distant past, families who chose to keep their children at home rather than placing them in residential institutions were subject to stigma. Now families are expected to raise their children with disabilities at home. Institutionalization is the exception rather than the rule, and families are expected to assume responsibilities associated with raising their children with special needs. Contrary to the earlier reality, present-day families who institutionalize children with disabilities are stigmatized, and families that choose to raise children with disabilities at home are highly visible.

Types of Family Involvement

It is popular these days to talk about family involvement. We regularly attend conferences at which we hear speakers calling for increased parent involvement and home–school collaboration as essential to solving problems that schools, students, and families face. Teachers tell us of the need to involve families in their children's education. Parents sometimes talk about their desire to participate in the education of their children. But what does family involvement mean?

There are at least five kinds of family involvement (Epstein, 1992). In the first, parents fulfill basic obligations, such as providing for their children's health and safety, getting them ready for school, and building the kind of home environment that supports learning. There is little contact with the school. In the second kind, the school creates certain minimal types of contact between school and family. The school communicates with parents about school programs, sends out report cards, and so on. In the third type, parents join activities at school by assisting the teacher and attending functions. A fourth kind is one in which parents participate in learning activities at home (e.g., they initiate learning activities or monitor completion of school-work). Finally, in the fifth, parents participate in governance and advocacy activities at school, including parent-teacher associations, parent study groups, and advocacy groups.

When professionals speak of increased family involvement, they generally mean at least the third of these five levels and often the fourth or fifth—involvement extensive enough that parents become genuine collaborators in their children's education.

Overcoming Barriers to Home–School Collaboration

Although professionals and families readily acknowledge the importance of working together, there are a number of barriers to home–school collaboration; some are listed in *Table 4.1*. To overcome these barriers, the school can do certain things to encourage family participation:

- Families are more likely to become involved in their children's educational programs if the school climate is open, helpful, and friendly. This can be accomplished by installing parent lounges and setting times when parents and teachers have lunch together, among other things.
- Parents are more likely to become involved in the educational program when there is frequent, clear, two-way communication. They are also more likely to communicate when they are encouraged to comment on school policies and issues and share in making decisions about programs.
- Parents are more likely to become involved when they are treated as collaborators rather than recipients of advice from experts. Active efforts must be made to involve parents, especially those who are considered hard to reach. Schools in which administrators actively express and promote a philosophy of partnership are likely to have high levels of family involvement. It is important to expect parents to work as volunteers, even after their children finish school.
- Schools should provide written policies about how teachers are to involve families in students' educational programs. Such documents might include statements of how families and teachers are to work together, the ways in which administrators support family involvement, how teachers are trained to work with families, ways to increase and improve two-way communication and networking, and methods for periodic evaluation of the effects of family involvement.

Some ways in which you as a professional will be able to work to overcome barriers to home–school collaboration follow:

- Send home good news as often as you send home bad news.
- Hold conferences with families beyond those that are routine and scheduled. Work to make such conferences nonroutine.
- Be sure to follow through on any communications with parents.

Table 4.1   Twelve Barriers to Effective Home-School
Collaboration

1. Parents feel anxious about surrendering their children to strangers who may have values different from their own and may inculcate in the children those values.

2. Teachers worry that parent involvement in decision making removes teacher independence and autonomy.

3. Sometimes teachers and parents will accede to their required responsibilities (as articulated by principals to diminish conflict and confusion); sometimes they will not.

4. Parents and teachers have inaccurate, often negative stereotypes of each other.

5. Because parents and teachers are busy, the pressure of having to get many things done in short periods of time interferes with effective collaboration.

6. Because many families have very low incomes, the financial pressures of making ends meet become primary to worrying about how their children are doing in school.

7. Parents are sometimes afraid to come to school because they do not view schools as safe environments.

8. Parents cannot always come to school because they cannot afford or have no access to child care for younger siblings.

9. School policies sometimes discourage home-school collaboration. For instance, in some schools, union contracts specify that volunteers cannot be used for teaching functions.

10. Teachers and parents hold different views on who ought to be in charge of major decisions.

11. Parents and teachers sometimes attribute student failure or poor performance to different, mutually exclusive factors, which sometimes means they blame each other.

(Continued)

Table 4.1 (Continued)

---

12. Many homes are socially stressed, and many students who experience difficulties in school are from socially stressed homes. The stresses may be such that they contribute to or exacerbate the difficulties students experience in school or take precedence over any difficulties students experience in school.

Sources: Henderson, A. T., Marburger, C. L., and Ooms, T. (1986). *Beyond the bake sale: An educator's guide to working with parents.* Washington, DC: National Committee for Citizens in Education. Imber-Black, E. (1992). *Families and larger systems.* New York: Guilford.

- Provide families with knowledge about how they can use your services, and ask parents to tell you how you can use them to further their children's education.
- Contact families by phone on a regular basis to let them know how their children are doing and to get their perceptions of how things are going in school. Work to reach those parents who tend to be unavailable, for it is precisely in such instances that obtaining family involvement has dramatic effects on student behavior and academic performance.

5

How Should Schools Involve Community Agencies and Businesses?

It is critical that transition services take into account the community in which the student will live. Students who live in rural environments will have different needs than those who live in inner-city or large urban environments. Various kinds and degrees of social services may be available in the different settings; therefore, it is important for those who plan transitions to coordinate the needs of the student with the availability of mechanisms and agencies for meeting those needs.

Students who receive special education services also come to the attention of other agencies and organizations. Services for students in the United States are provided by a bewildering array of federal, private, state, county, and city agencies and organizations. Services include education, health care, transportation, public assistance, housing, legal advice, and protection (fire and police). Collaboration between school personnel and those in other agencies is important so that "the right hand knows what the left is doing." Interagency collaboration can reduce redundancy of services and lead to improved benefits for students.

Over the years, agency personnel have become better at talking with one another and working together. Agencies are commonly more interdependent than independent. Teachers must work persistently to familiarize themselves with the services of agencies and the ways in which their personnel help students. Hodgkinson (1992) pointed to the ridiculous nature of failing to do so:

> It is painfully clear that a hungry, sick or homeless child is by definition a poor learner, yet schools usually have no linkage to health or housing organizations outside those run by the schools themselves. (p. 1)

Since Hodgkinson's (1989) observation, there have been major steps in the development of close linkages among schools and service organizations. Interagency collaboration is especially critical at the time that students make the transition from school to the postschool environment. Adult service agencies provide vocational, recreational, social, and mental health services. It is also important for school and agency personnel to work together early in students' schooling so that they can plan post-school life and facilitate transition.

BUSINESS INVOLVEMENT

Involvement of business leaders is also important. The basis for a highly skilled workforce begins in the school years, with a range of quality educational programs and work-related experiences that allow students to reach high school graduation equipped to tackle the world of work or to continue in some form of postsecondary education or training, or both. Wehman (1992) identified three reasons why it is important for school personnel to establish linkages with businesses and business leaders: First, local business personnel can help school personnel decide the extent to which the skills they are giving students are marketable. Second, businesses can serve as training sites for students, and business leaders can provide school personnel with analyses of the kinds of experiences they can offer students.

Finally, since businesses may eventually employ students with disabilities, it is important that school and business personnel understand one another.

Today's business leaders are working with education leaders to improve linkages. More and more communities are developing ways to help students prepare for the move from school to work. In most states, there are business partnerships designed to connect education, employment, work, and learning.

SPECIAL PROGRAMS

Students with disabilities participate in many of the programs that prepare all students for technical careers. Many of these students learn challenging academic material in real-world settings, where principles and ideas are applied to everyday problems and solutions. Programs that have resulted from close collaboration among educators and business leaders include youth apprenticeships, tech-prep programs, and school-based enterprises.

Youth Apprenticeships

Youth apprenticeships expose high school students to workday realities in areas such as health care, banking, insurance, hospitality, and retailing. Participants spend part of each school week at work sites and the remainder of the week in the classroom. The on-the-job emphasis is on active learning. The employment connections give students a chance to try out actual working situations and gain work experience.

Tech-Prep Programs

Tech-prep programs combine academic studies with job-related learning in a plan that links the final two years of high school with two years of college. People from industry join high school and community college teachers to develop curriculum, teach lessons, and monitor students at work sites. Students receive high-level training in math, science, language, and so forth and enough training in technical skills to integrate the two and assume demanding technical employment.

School-Based Enterprises

School-based enterprises are individual or sequenced high school courses set up as actual student-run businesses. Sandwich shops, bookstores, print shops, child care centers, and construction firms are among the enterprises. Students study business operations and develop occupational skills.

In these programs and others, communities are experimenting with programs that provide challenging academics, allow students to learn in context, and give them opportunities to explore and prepare for careers. Successful programs are built and maintained through close collaboration among teachers, parents, employers, and community leaders.

6

What Are the Keys to Success in the Wider Context?

As you think about the wider context of schooling for students who are exceptional, consider the key elements of effective instructional programs, whether for very young children in early intervention settings or young adults in supported work environments. Six elements have been found to increase the chances of success:

- Individualized planning
- Normal life experiences
- Compatibility with the physical environment
- Remedial programming
- Appropriate behavior
- Lifelong learning

Bringing Learning to Life: Community and Business Collaboration Facilitated Fred's Transition from School to Employment

Because of collaboration among his teachers, school administrators, state and county officials, and people from

(Continued)

(Continued)

the county technical college, Fred received substantial training in food services during his last two years of high school. Local business leaders were also involved in setting up this training program for students like Fred. Spending a few hours each day at the technical college, Fred learned vocational skills to give him a head start on finding employment after graduation.

Once Fred received his diploma, he was recommended for the McJobs program. Sponsored by the McDonald's chain of restaurants, McJobs is a structured eight-week training course for people with special needs. Since Fred had long envied people who worked at McDonald's, his favorite eating establishment, he jumped at the opportunity. He couldn't have been prouder when he got his uniform, especially the baseball-style cap.

He did well in McJobs, and he was hired as a regular employee at the local McDonald's. After a few months, the manager suggested that with training on more job stations, Fred could work more hours. The McJobs job coach spent an additional two weeks at the store to train Fred on additional job stations. He increased his work time to 32 hours a week at his dream job.

Fred's mother stated, "I never thought McDonald's would let Fred do as much as they have. He is a regular jack of all trades—he makes burgers, fries, nuggets, pies, everything in the grill area. He is now working breakfast as well as lunch, so he had to learn all those jobs too. When we got Fred, we were told that he was severely and profoundly retarded and would never walk, talk, or do anything. And now here he is supporting himself, and he loves his job."

INDIVIDUALIZED PLANNING

All services—from toilet training of young children in day care settings to job skills training and accommodations for adults—should be tailored to meet the specific needs of the individual. For example, if a young adult has difficulty with communication, detailed training in communication should be offered, including social skills training.

COMMITMENT TO NORMAL LIFE EXPERIENCES

The educational experiences of students who are exceptional should be as near to normal as possible. Specific efforts need to be made to help students with disabilities become integrated with their communities, whether in work environments or preschool programs.

COMPATIBLE PHYSICAL ENVIRONMENT

The physical environment at home, at work, and at school should be made compatible with the student's preferences. If noise disturbs the student, then efforts should be made to find a quiet place to educate him or her. Special considerations should be given to how the physical environment—layout, shape, noise level, location, and so on—affects the behavior of the individual.

COMMITMENT TO REMEDIAL PROGRAMMING

Even young children demonstrate uneven skill development and gaps in learning. The gaps evidenced by older students with disabilities often keep them from functioning independently. Educational services should be designed to teach new skills and to fill gaps in previously learned behavior or skills.

ENCOURAGING APPROPRIATE BEHAVIOR

Success in preschool, school, and work depends on the extent to which students demonstrate behaviors that others consider appropriate. Both early education and transition activities should be directed toward reduction of inappropriate behavior.

LIFELONG LEARNING

Students with disabilities will likely need support and assistance in learning throughout their lives. Consistency and adjustment in providing services is critical for all ages.

The education of students with disabilities is a lifelong effort that involves cooperation and collaboration among school personnel, parents and families, community agencies, religious organizations, and businesses. A significant part of education and development takes place before students enter school (**early intervention**) and after they leave (**post-school intervention**). Educators need to be concerned about this wider context and be actively involved in the transitions that occur in the lives of students with disabilities.

7

Working With Families and Agencies in Perspective

Transitions occur when students enter and leave school as well as during the school day. There are many efforts to intervene early in the lives of young children with disabilities, either to alleviate the disabilities or to prevent later and more significant difficulties. Although there are now more preschool programs than at any time in the history of the United States, significantly more children need early interventions. There is evidence that early intervention alleviates later school and developmental difficulties and that it results in improved outcomes for students, including those with disabilities. Educators ought to work hard to ensure full funding of Head Start and to provide preschool experiences to all children with disabilities. It is a good investment. Increased efforts to improve educational services for students with disabilities are needed in elementary and middle schools to decrease the currently large number of students who drop out of school. Waiting until high school to intervene is too late.

Educational outcomes for students with disabilities are not rosy. A large percentage drop out of school, most of those who complete school are unemployed or underemployed, and many work in sheltered workshops and supported employment settings rather than in competitive employment. This speaks to the need to improve educational services for these students but also the need to improve transition planning. By working with business and industry leaders, school personnel can engage in better transition planning.

There can be little doubt that improved educational outcomes for students with disabilities require improved instruction. Yet that is not enough; collaboration is equally necessary. Educators need to collaborate with one another in efforts to improve education for students with disabilities. They need to collaborate with families to forge strong linkages between home and school. They also need to collaborate with business and community leaders to develop ways to improve the results of education for students with disabilities. The significant challenges that confront students cannot be addressed by educators (or families, sociologists, psychologists, rehabilitation counselors, physicians and nurses, and so on) in isolation. Only by working together and working very hard can we improve educational outcomes for the nation's youth.

8

What Have We Learned?

As you complete your study of working with families and community agencies to support students with special needs, it may be helpful to review what you have learned. To help you check your understanding, we have listed the key points and key vocabulary for you to review. We have included the Self-Assessment again so you can compare what you know now with what you knew as you began your study. Finally, we provide a few topics for you to think about and some activities for you to do on your own.

KEY POINTS

More than half of 3- to 5-year-olds attend nursery school or kindergarten classes. Although there are more preschool programs than ever before, more students are in need of them.

Early intervention programs are home-based, center-based, or hospital-based.

◙ Transitions occur at the time of school entrance, during school (from grade to grade, elementary school to middle school, and general to special education), and at the time students leave school.

- A large proportion of students with disabilities—roughly one-quarter to one-third—drop out before school completion.

- When students with disabilities leave school, most are unemployed or underemployed.

- More students with disabilities work in sheltered and supported employment settings than in competitive employment.

- An increasing number of students with disabilities are continuing their education in colleges or other advanced schools.

- Many adults with disabilities live independently. The trend toward deinstitutionalization has promoted community living arrangements, such as group homes, alternative living units, and foster homes.

- There are at least five kinds of family involvement, ranging from parental fulfillment of basic obligations but little contact with the school to intense involvement in the schools their children attend. Teachers and other school personnel can help promote home–school collaboration.

- Business leaders, leaders from community agencies, and educational leaders increasingly have been working in partnership to improve educational outcomes for students with disabilities.

KEY VOCABULARY

Alternative living unit (ALU) is a supervised home for two or three exceptional students.

Center-based programs refers to programs in which parents bring their child to a hospital, day care center, clinic or other facility to receive direct or indirect services.

Community agency refers to an agency in the community which provides social services.

Competitive employment refers to employment in which the individual's work is valued by the employer and is performed in an integrated setting.

Deinstitutionalization is the movement of individuals from settings like hospitals and institutions into less restrictive, everyday environments.

Direct services refer to services provided directly to the child.

Early intervention refers to educational and other services provided before a child reaches school age or before school-related problems become serious.

Group homes are residences that provide family-style living for a group of exceptional people.

Head Start is a federal program providing preschool education for students who are economically disadvantaged; it is the best known early intervention program.

Home-based programs refer to instruction or tutoring in the homes of students unable to travel to school. Home-school collaboration refers to families and schools developing relationships as collaborative partners.

Hospital-based programs are special education programs provided to a student in a hospital or to hospital personnel who work with the student.

Indirect services refer to services that are provided to another person, such as parent, who in turn serves the child.

Individual family service plan (IFSP) details a child's present level of development, the family's needs related to that development, objectives of the program, specific services that will be provided to the child and family, evaluation procedures, and transition procedures to move the child from early intervention into a preschool program.

Individualized transition plan (ITP) is part of the individualized education program that specifies services to be provided to aid a student's transition from school to adult life.

Job coach is a professional who provides employment assistance in the form of on-the-job training and help to individuals with disabilities.

Least restrictive environment is an educational setting as much like the regular classroom as possible.

Mainstreaming means keeping exceptional students in the regular classroom whenever possible.

Post-school intervention refers to support and assistance for people with disabilities after they exit school.

School-based enterprises are high school courses or series of courses in which students operate their own businesses to learn occupational skills.

Sheltered employment is work in a self-contained environment in which the exceptional individual is trained and paid for output.

Supported employment uses professionals to help individuals with disabilities find, perform, and keep jobs.

Tech-prep programs combine academic study with job-related learning, linking the final two years of high school with two years of college.

Transition services refer to a set of coordinated activities for a student, designed within an outcome-oriented process, which promotes movement from school to post-school activities; it should be based upon the individual student's needs and take into account the student's preferences and interests.

Youth apprenticeship programs are those in which a student spends part of each school week in a classroom and the remainder at a work site to gain actual work skills and experience.

Self-Assessment 2

After you complete this book, check your knowledge and understanding of the content covered. Choose the best answer for each of the following questions.

1. As a result of the Public Law 98–199 passed in 1984, a child with special needs can receive comprehensive services

   a. From birth

   b. From the age of 1 year

   c. From the age of 2 years

   d. From the age of 3 years

2. What is the name of the federally funded early intervention program specially tailored for children from economically disadvantaged families?

   a. Success for All

   b. Head Start

   c. Hope for Every Child

   d. No Child Left Behind

3. The law requires that every child below the age of 5 years who has a disability have an

   a. Individualized life-stage plan

   b. Individualized transition plan

   c. Individualized education program

   d. Individualized family service plan

4. _____ services refer to services provided to the child in settings for early intervention programs.

   a. Direct

   b. Indirect

   c. Center-based

   d. Home-based

5. Which one of the following is NOT a student characteristic associated with a greater likelihood of students dropping out of school?

   a. Gender

   b. Learning style

   c. Size of the school

   d. Socioeconomic status

6. Which type of employment do professionals consider to be the goal of all young adults with disabilities?

   a. Full-time employment

   b. Sheltered employment

   c. Supported employment

   d. Competitive employment

7. Which one of the following is the term stated in the Education for All Handicapped Children Act that requires that children be placed in an educational setting as much like the regular classroom as possible?

   a. Deinstitutionalization

   b. Inclusion

   c. Least restrictive environment

   d. Mainstreaming

8. Which one of the following is viewed by professionals in special education as violating the ideal of "life as much like normal as possible" principle of the Individuals with Disabilities Act?

   a. Foster homes

   b. Group homes

   c. Residential institutions

   d. Alternative living units

9. _____ are programs which provide high school students exposure to actual working situations and the opportunity to gain work experience.

   a. Community transition program

   b. School-based enterprises

   c. Tech-prep programs

   d. Youth apprenticeships

10. The prevailing belief about students with disabilities is that

   a. Advanced schooling is too pressuring for them.

   b. They should strive to be as independent as possible.

   c. They should be placed in residential institutions as early as possible.

   d. They should work in self-contained environment specially tailored to their needs.

REFLECTION

After you answer the multiple-choice questions, think about how you would answer the following questions:

- What is early intervention? Why is it important to provide early intervention programs to children with special needs?
- What are the advantages and disadvantages of

  a. Home-based programs

  b. Center-based programs?

- What are the different forms of family involvement?
- How successful have you been encouraging family involvement in your school? What are some barriers to home–school collaboration? What can be done to overcome these barriers?

Answer Key for Self-Assessments

1. a

2. b

3. d

4. a

5. b

6. d

7. c

8. c

9. d

10. b

On Your Own

☑ Consult the Yellow Pages of your local phone directory for a list of preschool programs. Contact the programs to obtain informational brochures. Use the brochures to create a table with the name of each program, the age range of students, the kinds of students with disabilities included in the program, the organization of the program (e.g., home-based), and the kinds of services provided.

☑ Contact a teacher and discuss strategies school personnel can use to enhance family involvement in school programs. Indicate topics for small or large group meetings of parents.

☑ Develop a list of ways in which school personnel can work with high school seniors with disabilities to ensure smooth transitions from school to post-school environments.

☑ Develop a list of ways in which school personnel can work with individual preschool children to facilitate their smooth transition to school. Are there transition tactics that apply specifically to students with disabilities? Which tactics can be used with all students?

Resources

BOOKS

American Council on Rural Special Education. (1988). *Rural transition strategies that work.* Bellingham: Western Washington University, National Rural Development Institute. Designed to assist educators in establishing rural transition programs, this book describes over 50 exemplary transition programs, strategies, and practices tested in rural areas.

Christenson, S., & Sheridan, S. (2001). *Schools and families: Creating essential connections for learning.* New York: Guilford. This practical guide is designed to help school practitioners and educators build positive connections with families and enhance student achievement in grades K–12.

Dunst, C. J., Trivetta, C. M., & Deal, A. G. (1988). *Enabling and empowering families: Principles and guidelines for practice.* Cambridge, MD: Brookline. Written specifically for early intervention practitioners who work with families but who have not had extensive training in family systems assessment and intervention, this book offers ways to promote a family's ability to identify its needs and mobilize resources— strengthening family functioning.

Dunst, C.J., & Wolery, M. (1997). *Family policy and practice in early child care.* Greenville, CT: JAI. An analysis of family supportiveness of federal early care and education policy. Also includes a review of child care and preventing maltreatment.

National Center on Education and the Economy, and American Society for Training and Development. (1989). *Training America: Strategies for the nation.* Washington, DC: Author. This book provides background information on and recommendations for the development of a comprehensive strategy for improving job-related learning in the United States

Rosenberg, M. B. (1988). *Finding a way: Living with exceptional brothers and sisters.* New York: Lothrop, Lee, & Shepard. This is a sensitive, straightforward exploration of the feelings of three children from different families, each the brother or sister of a sibling with a disability.

Shonkoff, J. P. (2000). *From neurons to neighborhoods: The science of early childhood development.* Washington, DC: National Academy Press. A review of scientific evidence for the influence of environment on early childhood development.

Shonkoff, J. P., & Meisels, S. (Eds.). (2000). *Handbook of early childhood intervention.* Cambridge, UK: Cambridge University Press. This text includes both theoretical and practical articles describing interventions for young children.

Taylor, S. (1991). *Life in the community: Case studies of organizations supporting people with disabilities.* Baltimore: Brookes. This text provides strategies to respond to the unique needs of each learner and provide integrated classroom environments at the elementary and secondary levels. Included are guidelines for merging general and special education, preparing staff, involving families, encouraging student self-direction, managing classrooms, and structuring opportunities for collaboration.

West, L. L., Corbey, S., Boyer-Stephens, A., Jones, B., Miller, R. J., and Sarkees-Wircenski, M. (1992). *Integrating transition planning into the IEP process.* Arlington, VA: Council for Exceptional Children. This book helps educators assist students to make

smooth transitions from school to adult life by making sure
that skills for successful employment, community involvement, postsecondary education, leisure pursuits, and self-
advocacy are written into their IEPs.

Journals and Articles

Career Development for Exceptional Individuals, published by the
Division of Career Development, Council for Exceptional
Children (CEC), focuses on vocational, residential, and
leisure activities for children and adults with disabilities.
CEC, 1100 North Glebe Road, Suite 300, Arlington, VA
22201–5704; www.cec.sped.org

Early Education and Development, published by Psychological Press,
includes research and interventions in early education and
development. Early Education and Development, P. O. Box
328, Brandon, VT 05733–1007.

International Journal of Rehabilitation Research Quarterly is a quarterly journal focused on research studies in all areas relevant
to rehabilitation of individuals with disabilities. International
Society of Rehabilitation for the Disabled, Rehabilitation International, 432 Park Ave. South, New York, NY 10016; http://
gort.ucsd.edu/newjour

Journal of Early Intervention is the journal of the Division of Early
Childhood of the Council for Exceptional Children (CEC).
It is a multidisciplinary journal aimed at professionals work-
ing in special education and related fields. DEC, 1100 North
Glebe Road, Suite 300, Arlington, VA 22201–5704.

Topics in Early Childhood Special Education is published by Pro-Ed.
Each issue addresses a topic in early education and development. Pro-Ed, 8700 Shoal Creek Boulevard, Austin, TX
78757–6897; www.proedinc.com

ORGANIZATIONS

Association for the Care of Children's Health (ACCH)

An educational and advocacy organization, ACCH stresses the family's role in a child's life. With a membership of over 4,000, ACCH develops resources and training materials and cosponsors the National Information Clearinghouse for Infants with Disabilities and Life-Threatening Conditions. ACCH, 19 Mantua Rd., Mt. Royal, NJ 08061; www.acch.org

National Information Clearinghouse for Infants with Disabilities and Life-Threatening Conditions (NIC)

Established in 1986, NIC provides a national information and referral system for services pertaining to infants and young children with disabilities. NIC specialists help families and professionals access local and national services in such areas as early intervention, family support and training, assistive technology, and financial resources. NIC also produces bibliographies, fact sheets, monographs, and articles. NIC, Center for Developmental Disabilities, School of Medicine, Department of Pediatrics, University of South Carolina, Columbia, SC 29208.

National Information Center for Children and Youth with Disabilities (NICHCY)

NICHCY provides information and education on disability-related issues. NICHCY, P.O. Box 1492, Washington, DC, 20013; www.nichcy.org

References

Berrueta-Clement, J., Schweinhart, L., Barnett, S., Epstein, A., & Weikart, D. (1984). *Changed lives*. Ypsilanti, MI: High Scope Educational Foundation.

Committee for Economic Development. (1991). *The unfinished agenda: A new vision for child development and education*. Washington, DC: Author.

Currie, J., & Thomas, D. (1996). Does head start make a difference? *Network News & Views, 15*(4), 34–57.

Epstein, J. L. (1992). School and family partnerships: Leadership roles for school psychologists. In S. L. Christenson and J. C. Conoley (Eds.), *Home–school collaboration: Enhancing children's academic and social competence* (pp. 449–515). Silver Springs, MD: National Association of School Psychologists.

Haskins, R. (1989). Beyond metaphor: The efficiency of early childhood education. *American Psychologist, 44*, 274–282.

Henderson, A. T., Marburger, C. L., & Ooms, T. (1986). *Beyond the bake sale: An educator's guide to working with parents*. Washington, DC: National Committee for Citizens in Education.

Hodgkinson, H. L. (1992). *A demographic look at tomorrow*. Washington, DC: Center for Demographic Policy, Institute for Educational Leadership.

Imber-Black, E. (1992). *Families and larger systems*. New York: Guilford.

Individuals with Disabilities Education Act, Pub. L. No. 105–17, 111 Stat. 37 (1997).

Lee, V. E., Schnur, E., & Brooks-Gunn, J. (1988). Does Head Start work? A one-year follow-up comparison of disadvantaged children attending Head Start, no preschool, and other preschool programs. *Developmental Psychology, 24*(2), 210–222.

Mangrum, C., II, & Strichart, S. S. (1984). *College and the learning disabled student*. New York: Teachers College Press.

Mangrum, C., II, & Strichart, S. S. (1989). *College and the learning disabled student* (2nd ed.). Boston: Allyn & Bacon.

National Center for Education Statistics. (2002). *Early childhood education program participation: National household education surveys.* Washington, DC: Author.

National Institute for Early Childhood Education Research. (2002). *NIEER On-line News.* Piscataway, NJ: Rutgers University. Retrieved December 22, 2005, from http://nieer.org/resources/facts

Rusch, F., Chadsey-Rusch, J., & Lagomarcino, T. (1987). Preparing students for employment. In M. Snell (Ed.), *Systematic instruction of persons with severe handicaps* (3rd ed., pp. 471–490). Columbus, OH: Merrill.

Thurlow, M. L., Ysseldyke, J. E., Weiss, J. A., Lehr, C., O'Sullivan, P. J., & Nania, P. A. (1986). *Policy analysis of exit decisions and follow-up procedures in early childhood special education programs* (Research Report No. 14). Minneapolis: University of Minnesota, Early Childhood Assessment Project.

U.S. Department of Education. (1992). *Fourteenth Annual Report to Congress on the Implementation of the Individuals with Disabilities Education Act.* Washington, DC: Author.

U.S. Department of Education, Office of Special Education Programs. (2000). To assure the free appropriate public education of all children with disabilities. *Twenty-second annual report to Congress on the implementation of the Individuals with Disabilities Education Act.* Jessup, MD: Ed Pubs.

U.S. Department of Education, Office of Special Education Programs. (2002). To assure the free appropriate public education of all children with disabilities. *Twenty-fourth annual report to Congress on the implementation of the Individuals with Disabilities Education Act.* Jessup, MD: Ed Pubs.

Wagner, M. (1991, April). *School completion of students with disabilities: What do we know? What can we do?* Paper presented at the Annual Leadership Conference for State Directors of Special Education, Washington, DC.

Wagner, M., Blackorby, J., Cameto, R., Hebbeler, K., & Newman, L. (1993). *A summary of findings from the National Longitudinal Transition Study of Special Education Students.* Menlo Park, CA: SRI. Retrieved December 22, 2005, from www.sri.com

Wagner, M., D'Amico, R., Marder, C., Newman, L., & Blackorby, J. (1992). *What happens next? Trends in postschool outcomes for youth with disabilities: The second comprehensive report from the National Longitudinal Transition Study of special education students.* Menlo Park, CA: SRI.

Wehman, P. (1992). *Life beyond classrooms: Transition strategies for young people with disabilities.* Baltimore: Brookes.

Wilmington Morning Star. (June 2, 1988), p. 1C.

Index

Note: Numbers in **Bold** followed by a colon [:] denote the book number within which the page numbers are found.

Living arrangements, for adults
with special needs
alternative living unit, **5:**31
foster homes, **5:**31–32
group homes, **5:**30–31
independent living, **5:**32
institutions, **5:**33
Lloyd, J., **4:**40
Logical errors, **3:**62
Long, E., **12:**67
*Lora v. New York City Board of
Education,* **2:**40 (tab)–41 (tab)
Loudness, **7:**19–20, **7:**60
Louisiana Department of
Education, **13:**12
Low vision, **7:**60–61
Luckner, J., **7:**24, **7:**38,
7:42, **7:**50
Luetke-Stahlman, B.,
7:24, **7:**42, **7:**50
Lynch, E. W., **8:**56–58,
8:57 (tab)

Mainstreaming, **2:**54, **2:**56,
5:29–30, **5:**56
See also Least restrictive
environment
Mangrum, C. II, **5:**26
Manifestation determination,
2:29, **2:**56
Manual movements, **7:**40, **7:**61
Marburger, C. L., **5:**42 (tab)
Marder, C., **5:**24
Marland, S., **13:**41–42
Maryland State Department of
Education, **13:**11
Mastery, defining, **9:**32
Mathematics, improving,
6:27, **9:**32–33, **9:**34 (fig)
McBurnett, K., **9:**44
McKinney, J. D., **9:**51
McMeniman, M. M., **4:**5
Measures of process disorders,
9:18–19

Medical disabilities, **8:**9–16
AIDS, **8:**12–13
cystic fibrosis, **8:**12
fetal alcohol syndrome, **8:**14
heart conditions, **8:**12
hemophilia, **8:**13–14
identification by medical
symptoms, **8:**9–10
maternal cocaine use, **8:**14–15
medically fragile/technology
dependent groups,
8:15–16
other health impairments,
8:10–11 (tab)
prevalence of, **8:**10
special health problems,
8:14–15
Medical procedures, to ensure
appropriate education,
2:46, **2:**48, **2:**54
Medical treatment, for emotional
disturbance, **11:**37–38
Medically fragile, **8:**15, **8:**64
Medical/physical/multiple
disabilities
academic characteristics
of, **8:**38
behavioral characteristics of,
8:39–40
cognitive characteristics of,
8:37–38
communication characteristics
of, **8:**40–41
distribution of child with,
8:7–8 (fig)
home *vs.* institutional care for,
8:55–56
inclusion of student with, **8:**56
inclusion of student with,
overcoming barriers to,
8:56–59, **8:**57 (tab)
medical disabilities, **8:**9–16,
8:10–11 (tab)
multiple disabilities, **8:**33–35

National Commission on
  Excellence in Education,
  6:19–20
National Council on Educational
  Standards and Testing,
  6:31–32
National Dissemination Center
  for Children with
  Disabilities (NICHY),
  11:44–46
National Education Goals,
  5:10, **6**:19–20, **6**:45
National Educational
  Standards and
  Improvement Council, **6**:31
National Governors'
  Association, **6**:20, **6**:34
National Head Injury
  Foundation (NHIF), **8**:27–28
National Information Center,
  10:38
National Institute on Deafness
  and Other Communication
  Disorders Information
  Clearinghouse, **7**:58
National Joint Committee on
  Learning Disabilities
  (NJCLD), **9**:15, **9**:50
National Research Council, **1**:13
Nechita, A., **1**:35
Needs assessments, **4**:41, **4**:64
Nephrosis/nephritis,
  8:11 (tab), **8**:65
Neurological disorders, **8**:22–25
  cerebral palsy, **8**:23–24
  epilepsy, **8**:23
  overview of, **8**:25 (tab)
  spina bifida, **8**:24
  spinal cord injury, **8**:24–25
Newland, T. E.,
  7:12–13, **7**:30
Newman, L., **5**:24
NHIF (National Head Injury
  Foundation), **8**:27–28

NICHY (National Dissemination
  Center for Children with
  Disabilities), **11**:44–46
NJCLD (National Joint
  Committee on Learning
  Disabilities), **9**:15, **9**:50
No Child Left Behind Act, **2**:12
  (tab), **2**:29–31, **2**:54, **6**:10,
  6:37–38, **6**:45
Nonattention (distractibility),
  11:29–30, **11**:47
Noncategorical, **12**:18, **12**:71
Noncompliance (oppositional
  behavior), **11**:22–24, **11**:47
Nonmanual movements,
  7:40, **7**:61
Nonphysical disruptions,
  11:27–28, **11**:47
Normal field of vision, **7**:9, **7**:61
Normalization, **12**:61, **12**:72
Normative peer comparisons,
  4:28, **4**:64
Norm-referenced tests, **3**:29, **3**:80,
  4:9, **4**:64
Norms, **3**:8–9, **3**:80
Nystagmus, **7**:10, **7**:61

Objective-referenced test. *See*
  Criterion-referenced tests
Observations, **3**:25–26, **3**:29–30
  active, **3**:29, **3**:77
  defining, **3**:80
  formal, **3**:29
  informal, **3**:27, **3**:29, **3**:44
  language, **3**:44
  of achievement, **3**:38
  of sensory acuity, **3**:40–41
  passive, **3**:29, **3**:80
  perceptual-motor, **3**:48
Occupational and
  social skills, **3**:42
OCR (Optical character
  recognition), **7**:36 (tab),
  7:38, **7**:61

**CORWIN
PRESS**

The Corwin Press logo—a raven striding across an open book—represents the union of courage and learning. Corwin Press is committed to improving education for all learners by publishing books and other professional development resources for those serving the field of PreK–12 education. By providing practical, hands-on materials, Corwin Press continues to carry out the promise of its motto: **"Helping Educators Do Their Work Better."**